IT'S ALL LOVE OVER THERE

PALMETTO
PUBLISHING
Charleston, SC
www.PalmettoPublishing.com

Copyright © 2024 by Ashur Cordes

All rights reserved
No portion of this book may be reproduced, stored in a retrieval system, or transmitted in any form by any means–electronic, mechanical, photocopy, recording, or other.

Paperback ISBN: 979-8-8229-5708-4

IT'S ALL LOVE OVER THERE

An awesome account of unconditional love

ASHUR CORDES

IT'S ALL LOVE OVER THERE
My near death experience

The true God and religion are not one and the same.

This is a brief account of what it was like for me on the other side. My first-hand experience in the two hospitals, and the experiences afterward, reveal the awesome love and provision that are continually made for us by the Cross.

I had an emergency heart by-pass surgery followed by very serious complications. The medical staff had no choice but to operate without delay, at a time when I was on a full prescription of Plavix plus another blood thinner. The left main artery was described as 98% closed. I may not have been able to live a week.

Surgery was scheduled right away. After surgery, they could not stop the bleeding. My medical records show that I lost 18 pints or units of blood those first hours after surgery. They were unable to wake me even 10 hours after the normal wake up time. I was getting weaker and the blood loss accelerated to two and one half times the original rate. They could no longer keep up with the blood loss and they told my family, "We've done all we can for him. You should prepare for the inevitable; he's probably only got about 15 minutes to live." The nurse said, "Only prayer will save him now."

One of my three sons is a police officer in a densely populated area. He has seen more dead people than he cares to remember. He said that when he saw me after surgery I was the color of a dead person. I was unconscious, of course, with all that blood loss.

There were over thirty inches of cuts on my body since veins from my arm and leg were removed to do the bypass. The primary vein from my other arm had collapsed, so blood was given to me through my carotid artery to keep my brain and heart alive during the severe blood loss.

This was on a weekend when there was an unusual amount of emergency surgeries, and they ran out of blood that was compatible with mine. I do not have the most common blood type, and suddenly they were out. When the nurse told my family that they could not keep up with the blood loss, my two wonderful daughters-in-law offered to direct transfuse blood from themselves to save my life. They had the same blood type as mine. The hospital refused, even though they had stated that I only had about 15 minutes to live, at the present rate of loss. It was against their policy. That left just one option: PRAYER!

I remember, at the lowest point, looking down at my body from eight feet above. It was discolored with head drooped to one side. I thought, "If I keep a cool head like a wounded deer I will lose less blood and may live." Then nothing happened and I realized I was getting worse. I could feel the great stress of not being able to breathe. Thirty seconds went by and still no air. I thought, "I will grit my teeth and bear it for at least a minute and just deal with the suffocation." Then it became unbearable! The misery of that moment was beyond words, so I said the only thing that made any sense to me. I said, "Jesus! Where are You?" And instantly He said, "I'm right here in the darkness." And He rushed in and hugged me, and all the pain and stress were gone. (This took about 1/10th of a second.) As He took the agony, pain, and suffocation away from me, He said, "I bore that suffocation on the Cross, so you do not have to." (bear it). His love was all encompassing! It totally permeated me and everything around me—TOTAL LOVE, TOTAL ACCEPTANCE!

You may ask, "How do you know it was Jesus who answered you?" Believe me, when your time comes, you will absolutely know who shows up! I was surprised He accepted me.

I could see that I was going to Heaven, and I felt that I did not deserve it. I asked, "What about my sin?" I was looking around for it. (I remembered asking for forgiveness just before losing consciousness, but I did not think that was deserving of having my sins forgiven.) Jesus said, "Your sin was taken care of at the Cross." I saw the verse, John 3:16 written on His chest.

When I experienced what I have described, I was inside a ball of light about eight feet above my body. Surrounding that light was soft, silky darkness. When Jesus showed up, immediately after I asked for Him, there was no fear, just love, acceptance, forgiveness, and no condemnation. He conveyed that He wanted to be with me and other human souls as an integral highest wish to be one with The Father and The Holy Spirit, His original family. It seemed like we had always belonged together, like I had been on a journey and was going back home.

I didn't see His face, but I saw His lower two thirds. He was wearing a pure white robe with purple and gold down the side, and a very large gold belt around His waist. On His clothing, on His chest, was the verse, John 3:16, in the King James Version: "For God so loved the world that He gave His only begotten son, that whosoever believes in him should not perish, but have everlasting life." The main emphasis is that all of us who believe that verse will make it to Heaven.

Then, as I was looking down at my body, I saw my family come in and encircle my bed. They prayed. Then Dad was there too! (Dad and Mom had passed on years earlier.) There was gold light coming from him. He appeared to be in his thirties. Mom was to the right of my head. She seemed to be about twenty-five years old.

I was given the choice of going to Heaven or coming back. I chose to come back because I wanted to see my grandchildren. I knew Jesus was eternal. It was more fun being with Jesus than going to Heaven, and I knew He would never leave me. As my family prayed around my bed, I also heard, or became aware of prayers coming in from many different places. I heard prayers from a Baptist Church, a ladies' prayer chain, two Full Gospel Churches, a group of Catholic believers, a church in England, one in Tennessee, prayers from Arizona, and from my pastor. All this after the nurse had said, "Only prayer will save him now."

As I was looking down at my body, I heard the pastor say, "Lord, we need a miracle!" I saw my son's mother-in-law praying with my sister, several miles away. They prayed, "Lord, make the doctor's hands become Your hands!" I quoted the prayer back to them later. They were amazed because they had not told anyone what they had prayed.

The doctors were going to open my chest again in an attempt to stop the bleeding. Before they started, I heard a medical staff member say, "We're out of blood. There is more being flown in." "How long will that take?" "half an hour" "That will be too late!"

Then I heard an order from Jesus that all prayers be answered and the bleeding stop. A huge hand appeared under my bed, and a gold light surrounded it. I saw the healing happen from eight feet above my body. Jesus took all the prayers in His large, kind hands and funneled them into my heart, and all the bleeding stopped. Then a crystal stream of water came from Him and went into my head, and I was inside my body again!

The doctors didn't hear that order. When they opened my chest for the second time, the records show, in their own writing, there was no bleeding and corrective surgery was no longer necessary. Their report confirms I was healed.

This all seems like foolishness to people who have decided not to believe. All of the people I've told about this experience have believed me except one. He said, "You sound like you are crazy!" I wanted him to realize that, if we serve a living God, all good things are available to us. Unfortunately, two months after I told him, he very unexpectedly died. It was the second time, in a few short years, he had rejected what I had to tell him of God's healing grace.

In closing, when Jesus hugs you, it is like you are being hugged everywhere, even at the cellular level. Total love and physical + emotional comfort permeates every cell of your body and all the spaces in between.

All of you is hugged and loved beyond description. It feels like unconditional love.

A person's emotional and psychological hurts and scars are finally and completely healed as well.

You become a new and whole person, and the love stays with you.

All you have to do is believe in Jesus. For example: see John 3:16.